People
in My Neighborhood

by Shelly Lyons

Consulting editor: Gail Saunders-Smith, PhD

CAPSTONE PRESS
a capstone imprint

Pebble Plus is published by Capstone Press,
1710 Roe Crest Drive, North Mankato, Minnesota 56003
www.capstonepub.com

Library of Congress Cataloging-in-Publication Data
Lyons, Shelly.
People in my neighborhood / by Shelly Lyons.
p. cm. — (Pebble plus: my neighborhood)
ISBN 978-1-62065-099-8 (library binding)
ISBN 978-1-62065-883-3 (paperback)
ISBN 978-1-4765-1722-3 (ebook PDF)
1. Neighborhoods—Juvenile literature. 2. Neighbors—Juvenile literature. I. Title.
HT152.L96 2013
307.3'362—dc23   2012023416

Editorial Credits
Sarah Bennett, designer; Svetlana Zhurkin, media researcher; Kathy McColley, production specialist

Photo Credits
Alamy: Frances Roberts, 21; Capstone Studio: Karon Dubke, 7, 17, 19; Getty Images: Symphonie, 5; iStockphotos: kali9, 13; Shutterstock: Alexander Raths, 15, A-R-T (background), 1 and throughout, Monkey Business Images, 11, Rob Marmion, cover, Thomas M. Perkins, 9

Note to Parents and Teachers

The My Neighborhood set supports social studies standards related to community. This book describes and illustrates people in a neighborhood. The images support early readers in understanding the text. The repetition of words and phrases helps early readers learn new words. This book also introduces early readers to subject-specific vocabulary words, which are defined in the Glossary section. Early readers may need assistance to read some words and to use the Table of Contents, Glossary, Read More, Internet Sites, and Index sections of the book.

Printed in the United States   5989

Table of Contents

Who Are Your Neighbors?

Neighbors are people

who live near us.

They are people we should

get to know.

Helping Neighbors

A family is moving

into the house next to Lisa's.

They will be Lisa's

new neighbors.

She says hello and helps out.

Lexi lives next door to

Mr. Barnes.

She helps him plant flowers.

Neighbors Who Teach

Ms. Hon teaches art

at the community center.

She helps neighborhood

children make art projects.

Jaden spots Mr. Janke.

Mr. Janke is a librarian.

He helps Jaden find

books about dinosaurs.

Neighbors Who Serve

Ms. Jackson is a doctor

at the clinic down the street.

She enjoys helping people

feel better.

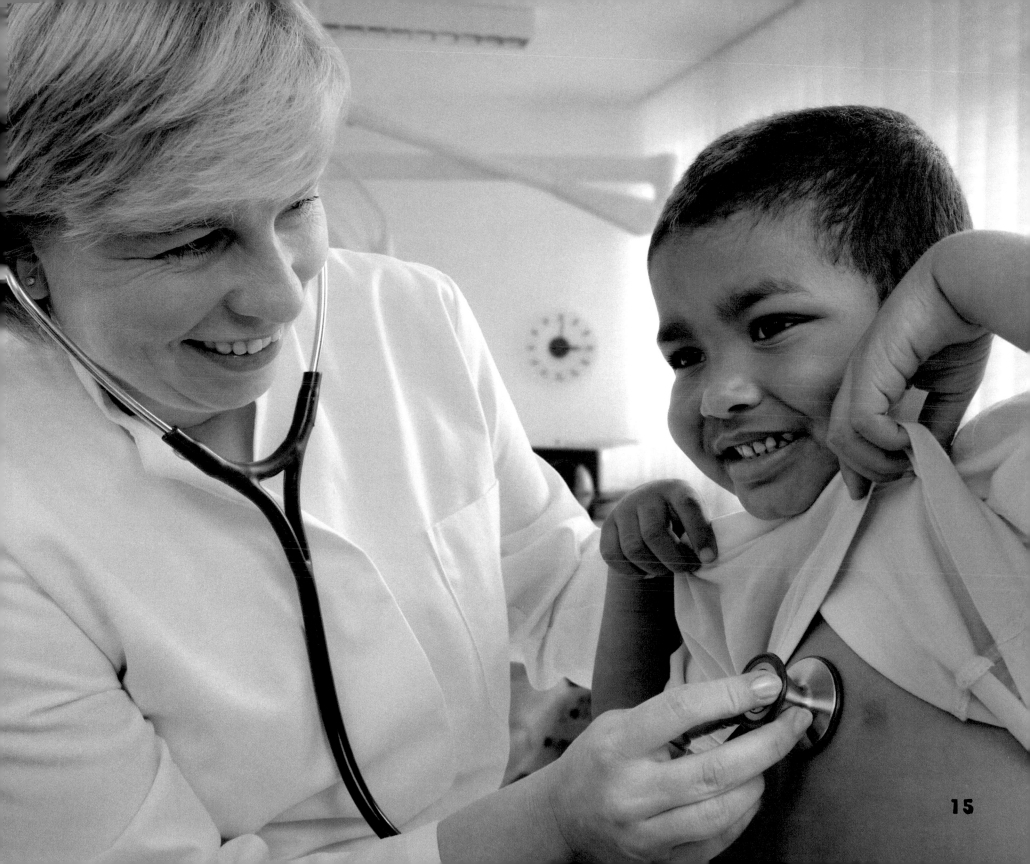

Ms. Adams is a police officer.
She talks to Mark about safety
in the neighborhood.

Lila and Max visit a firefighter
at the fire station.
Mr. Michaels teaches them
about fire safety.

We see neighbors every day.

Each one is special.

How can you get to know

your neighbors?

FRESH 50¢
Lemonade/Orange

50¢
CUP

Glossary

clinic—a building where people go to receive medical care; some doctors have offices in clinics

community—a group of people who live in the same area

neighbor—someone who lives in the same area

neighborhood—a small area in a town or city where people live

police officer—someone who is trained to make sure people obey the law

project—a plan or activity

station—a building where a certain service is based

Read More

Brown, Tameka Fryer. *Around Our Way on Neighbors' Day.* New York: Abrams Books for Young Readers, 2010.

Crabtree, Marc. *Meet My Neighbor, the Police Officer.* Meet My Neighbor. New York: Crabtree Pub., 2012.

Schuette, Sarah L. *Communities.* People. Mankato, Minn.: Capstone Press, 2009.

Internet Sites

FactHound offers a safe, fun way to find Internet sites related to this book. All of the sites on FactHound have been researched by our staff.

Here's all you do:

Visit *www.facthound.com*

Type in this code: 9781620650998

Super-cool stuff! Check out projects, games and lots more at **www.capstonekids.com**

Index

Word Count: 146
Grade: 1
Early-Intervention Level: 16